Dimes to Teach Your Child About Money

by Rebecca D. Turner

Illustrations: Mike Motz

Book design: www.EssexGraphix.com
Editor: Mike Motz

Cutting Edge Publishing
P.O. Box 470062
Fort Worth, TX 76147

www.readdimes.com

ISBN: 978-0-692-21728-3

Printed in Canada

Contents

Asher and Jordyn Ann were friends who lived in the same neighborhood and were going to attend the same school. They had known each other since they were little and had attended day care and preschool together.

Asher lived with his mom, dad, and sister, Cassidy. Jordyn Ann lived with her Aunt Bonnie and their dog, Finnegan.

Asher had a new lunch box for his first day of school, and Jordyn Ann had a new red top that her Aunt Bonnie bought her to wear on her first day of school.

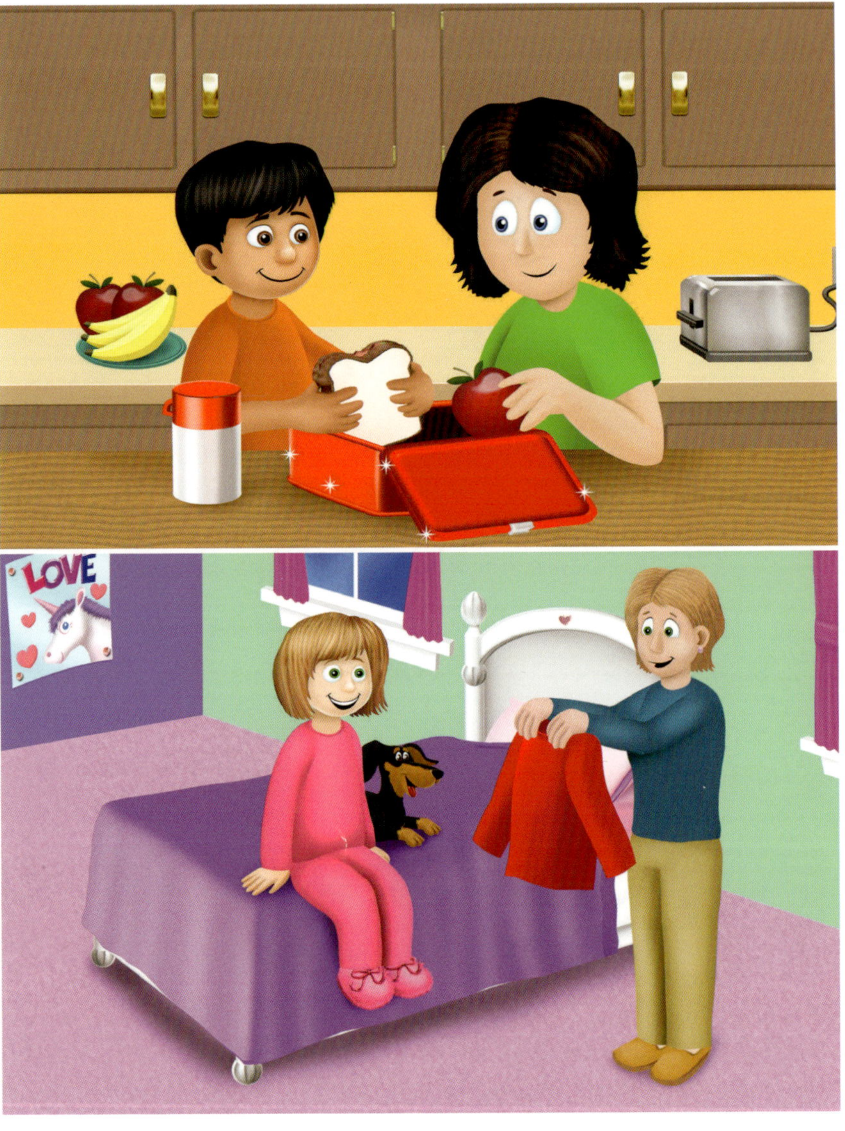

Jordyn Ann was excited to meet her new teacher and wondered if her friends would like her new top. Asher couldn't wait to see his friends again and meet his new teacher.

When Asher and Jordyn Ann went to their first day of school they met their teacher. When they met her she said “Hello, my name is Mrs. Harkey, and I am excited that you will be in my class this year.”

Mrs. Harkey had asked Asher's dad, who was a banker, to come and talk to the class about money. He said that Mrs. Harkey had a project for them that would last all year, and it would teach them about saving, investing, taxes, and giving. The project was to help them understand money.

"Wow," Asher thought, "a project that started the very first day of school that would last all year!" Asher could not wait to get home and go to the store to buy the items he needed for the project. Jordyn Ann could not wait to tell her Aunt Bonnie about the project and her first day of school.

The materials that Asher and Jordyn Ann needed for their project were four clear jars with metal lids; blue, green, red and orange colored markers; and four labels.

On the first label, Asher and Jordyn Ann wrote the word "save" with their blue markers. On the second, they wrote "invest" in green, while the third had "tax" in red marker. On the last label, they each wrote "give" in orange. When they were done, they placed one label on each of the four clear jars. With the help of an adult, they cut a slot in the top of each lid.

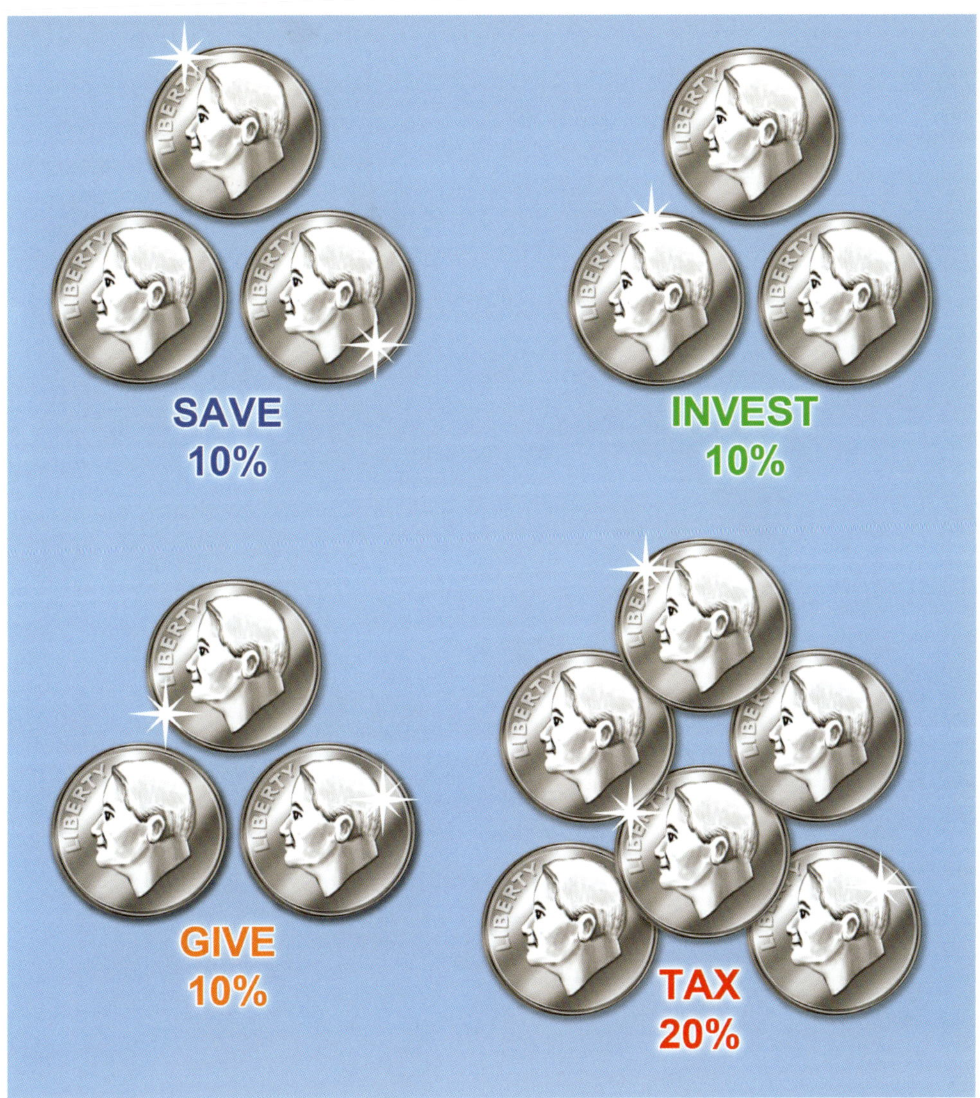

On the first of each month, their family would give them each thirty dimes. They had to put ten percent (three dimes) in each of the "save," "invest," and "give" jars; while twenty percent (six dimes) were to be put into the "tax" jar. That left fifteen to spend now on whatever they wanted. Mrs. Harkey asked everyone to think about to whom they would want to give the "give" dimes, and on what they would like to spend their "save" money. They would have a whole year to decide.

Saving would be money that they collected all year, and then they could buy something they wanted at the end of the year. Investing would be for money to put away for a very long time. Taxes would be kept all year, and then given back to the person who gave them the money each month. Giving would be saved, and then at the end of the year they would give the money to someone or something, like a zoo, who needed it.

At the end of the year, the dimes in their "save," "invest," and "give" jars would be traded for one dollar for each dime in the jars.

Asher thought that he would use his "save" money to buy a new set of headphones so that he could listen to his favorite music. Jordyn Ann wanted to buy a new sports car for her doll to drive.

For their "give" money, Asher had heard people at church say that they were saving money to build a new building, so he wanted to give his money to his church. Jordyn Ann thought that she would give it to the local pet shelter because she really loved animals, especially dogs.

Every month, when Asher's mom and dad, and Jordyn Ann's Aunt Bonnie gave them the thirty dimes, they would go right away and put them in their jars. They talked about how fun it was, since the jars were clear, to see the dimes build up. They remembered to put three dimes in each of the "save," "invest," and "give" jars and six dimes in the "tax" jar. Of course, then they had the fifteen dimes that were left for them to spend!

Before they knew it, the school year was almost over and they had three more months to wait and finish their money project. Mrs. Harkey asked Asher's dad to come back and talk to the class again right before school was out for the summer. They had learned a lot in class that year, so they reviewed what they would do with their dimes at the end of summer. Mrs. Harkey asked each student again how they planned to spend their "save" dimes, and to whom they would donate their "give" dimes.

Asher's dad informed the class that the money in their "invest" jar could be put into a savings account or college savings plan at his bank. He said that he could talk to their families about how to do this with the money that they were saving all year. This money would be put away for a long long time, and could be used for college or special things they needed when they were older. He also reminded the class that the dimes in their "tax" jar would all have to be given back to their family—the people who had helped them with their project.

Asher and Jordyn Ann talked about how hard it was to not take any money out of the jars. They also talked about how during the summer months of the money project, it was harder and harder for them not to take money out of their jars. Asher and Jordyn Ann knew that once school started again they would go back to Mrs. Harkey's class and report on their money project.

Asher had a friend named Liam who lived with his mom, dad, and sisters, Brooke and Emilie. That summer he found out that Liam's house had burned down, and all of his family's belongings were gone. Asher and his dad went to see the house after they heard that it had burned down. Asher had never seen a burned down house before.

When they walked around the corner to Liam's house, Asher could not believe what he saw! Liam's whole house was gone, and the only thing left was the porch where they had played!

All year Asher had been planning to give his money to his church, since they wanted to build a new building, but as they walked back to their house Asher asked his dad what he thought about giving his money to Liam instead of the church. Asher's dad said he thought that was a great idea, and that he was very proud of him for thinking of Liam who had lost everything.

At the end of the summer, when it was time to finish their project, Asher and Jordyn Ann were excited to see how many dimes they had in each of the jars. They could not believe how many dimes had built up in the "tax" jar that they had to give back to their families. After all, they were putting twice as many dimes in the "tax" jar every month!

Aunt Bonnie took Jordyn Ann to the pet shelter to give them the money that she had collected all year. Since there were twelve months where Jordyn Ann had put in three dimes a month, she had thirty-six dimes in her "give" jar. She took the dimes and traded them for thirty-six one-dollar bills that she wanted to give to the pet shelter.

As Jordyn Ann walked out of the pet shelter, she was amazed at how good it felt to give the money to the shelter so that they could help the animals and give them a place to live until they found a good home. She told Aunt Bonnie that she loved animals very much, and that when she grew up she wanted to be a veterinarian so that she could help even more animals!

When Asher's grandma, Esther, heard that he had saved money all year that he would invest in a college savings plan, she decided to contribute to his college as well. She told Asher that she would match every dollar that he invested with three dollars of her own money. Asher had saved thirty-six dollars, and adding $108 from his grandma would give him $144 to start his college savings plan. Wow! Asher didn't know about college or what that was about, but he really thought it was pretty neat that Grandma Esther wanted to help him invest for his future, too.

Later that day, Asher went with his dad to meet Liam and his family. Asher had put the thirty-six dollars from the dimes that he traded his dad into an envelope with Liam's name written on it. He knew that Liam had lost all of his toys and clothes, and that Liam's sisters, Brooke and Emilie, had lost all of their things, too. Asher knew that the money could not replace everything, but he thought that Liam could at least buy a few new things, and maybe even something for his sisters, too.

Asher felt really good about giving the money to his friend Liam. He talked with his dad as they walked home, and he told him that what happened to Liam and his family made him decide that he wanted to grow up to be a fireman.

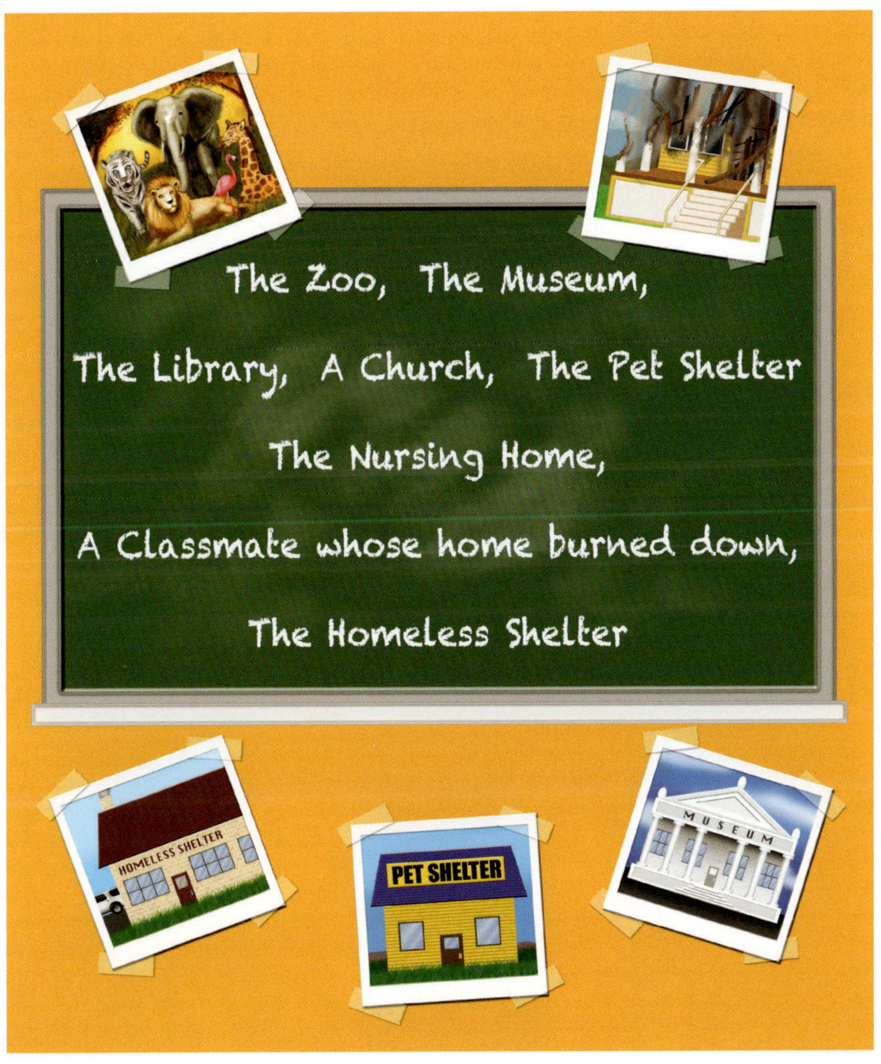

It had been a whole year since they started their money project, which meant it was time to go back to school! Mrs. Harkey had asked Asher's class to come back and talk to the new students about the project, and to write on the chalkboard where they gave the money that they had saved. The students had given to the zoo, a museum, their church, a homeless shelter, a nursing home, the pet shelter, and to a friend who lost his house. They thought it was fun getting to tell the younger class about what they had done.

Asher and Jordyn Ann could not believe everything they learned from their project. They not only saved to buy something they really wanted, but they were able to invest money that they could use when they were older and give money where it was really needed.

With their money project behind them, Asher and Jordyn Ann were excited and imagined what lay ahead.

A Tribute

On April 21, 2012, I lost my youngest nephew, Jordan, in an automobile accident. He was nineteen years old. He graduated from high school and started a small ship and print business. He had dreamed of getting married and starting a family. I'll never understand the "why" behind his death; someone so young with a life cut so short. In contrast, I have been able to do and see so much in my life and the blessings I have had seem so unfair. Jordan was one of the sweetest kids and human beings I have ever known. Pets had a real affinity for him. They wanted to be near him as if they sensed how sweet he was, and he loved them back.

When I was trying to find names for the kids in my new book, I looked up names for girls that were predicted to be what people used for the future. I liked many of the boy names, but none of the girl names really spoke to me. I then decided that I would use the female name of Jordan, Jordyn as a tribute to him. Ann is a family name with several women in my family who use Ann as a middle name.

After Jordan passed away, I felt the need to write something for him that comforted me and let others know how special he was.

Sweet Jordan

I believe pets can see through to the depths of our soul.
When we are honest and good, then they let us know.
They go to the ones, sweet, gentle and kind.
In you a faithful, comforting friend they did find.
Now we all have our challenges,
in some of us they don't show, but in other's they do,
Some people may have seen the challenges in you.
But for those who knew you deep down inside,
You were Jordan the gentle, sometimes funny and very kind.
You had so many feelings and to show them you weren't afraid.
The joys you didn't get to experience, I wish I could trade.
As your untimely death makes us greatly aware,
Life often stings, and it is definitely not fair.
It could drive us crazy comprehending the "why."
Let us look to God, and not even try.
Though we won't know the when, why or how.
Please go and save a place for us now.
Wait for us, for our time will come,
And you can greet us there and welcome us home.
As we search for our peace, and learn to let go of the "why,"
For you sweet Jordan, be free, you have your peace - you can fly.

Mrs. Harkey

The other name in the book that is a tribute is Mrs. Harkey. Mrs. Harkey was a kindergarten teacher at Belle Isle Elementary School in Oklahoma City, Oklahoma. Over her thirty year career, hundreds of kids experienced her classroom and were influenced by her. Just a few years ago, as she was attending to her husband in the hospital, she encountered a doctor whom she had in her kindergarten class. I believe many of us have a "Mrs. Harkey" in our past; that one special teacher when we were young that inspired us and even motivated us to want to be successful at something in life. So Mrs. Harkey is a tribute to her and those she influenced, as well as the rest of us and our own "Mrs. Harkey."

Why Dimes

Several years ago I had read in *Jesus Life Coach* by Laura Beth Jones about having a love relationship with God. At the time, I was going through a really low time in my life and after reading about how the author had a relationship with God that when she saw something special, it reminded her God was there. I had prayed about a relationship like that with God and myself. The author talked about how sometimes God seems far away, and so whenever God wanted to remind her that He was around, to show a ladybug to her. She had seen a ladybug land on her computer as she was working on her book manuscript inside of a hotel room in New York City.

When I finished that part of the book, I prayed to God that He seemed far away to me too, and that I would like to have that kind of relationship as well. I had read the book *The Power of Intention* by Robert W. Dyer and read an affirmation one morning that stated, "You are a person who acquires and attracts wealth." After I read that, I was walking my dogs and found a dime on the sidewalk. I thought it was kind of funny as a way for God to tell me He had heard me, but with a sense of humor since a dime is a small way to "start." Because of that experience and the ten percent we are to tithe, I decided on seeing a dime as my omen. That very day I saw a dime all by itself on the ground. Since then (which was 2004), I have seen hundreds of dimes. I now keep them in a book and write what I am going through at the time. They are reminders that God is here and thinks of me. Since dimes are special to me, I get excited when I find them. I have found many in odd places. I found one in particular between the wooden armrests in a theatre in New York City during a performance of Wicked. The humorous detail was that it was a Canadian dime. I again saw God's sense of humor, as if he was saying, "Does this count?"

When I decided to write a kids book about money, I had to choose the form of currency for the kid's project. This is one reason I chose dimes.

I would like to thank first my Lord and savior Jesus Christ. Malissa Turner for believing in me, encouraging me and for advice on this project. Lacey Braziel for her impeccable attention to detail and help organizing and editing this project. Fannye Rangel for her help in servicing our clients. Stacy Luecker with Essex Graphix for creating my website, typesetting the book and the cover design. Mike Motz for his illustrating and editing help.

About Rebecca

Education

- Wharton Certificate in Retirement Planning, Wharton School, University of Pennsylvania (2007-present)
- Chartered Financial Consultant (ChfC), The American College, Bryn Mawr, PA (1994-present)
- Kansas State University, 1985 B.A.

Community Involvement

- Financial advisor in the DFW area since 1989
- Published in *Builder Architect* magazine and *The Image* (a NAWIC publication)
- "An Evening of Hope" Chair, benefitting AIDS Outreach Center, 2010
- YWCA Tribute to Women in Business Honoree, 2008
- Tarrant County College "Visions Unlimited" Speaker
- Published author: *Tattoo* (2006), *Virus* (2008), Psych (2011), *Chosen: An Adoption Story* (2011)
- Recognized as one of the Great Women of Texas, 2003
- Leadership Fort Worth, Class of 1999
- National Association of Women in Construction (Former President, 2000-2001)
- American Cancer Society Sword of Hope Award, 1995

ORDER FORM

To order additional copies of this book,
or copies of *Chosen: An Adoption Story,*
please visit online at

www.readdimes.com

Fill out the order form and fax

817-806-3592

or mail this form and $19.95 + $3 s/h to

Cutting Edge Publishing
P.O. Box 470062
Fort Worth, TX 76147

(please print)

Name ____________________

Address ____________________

City ____________ State ______ Zip ______

Phone ____________________

E-mail ____________________

Payment method

❏ Check ❏ Money Order ❏ Credit Card

❏ VISA ❏ M/C ❏ AMEX ❏ Discover

Credit card number ____________________

Expiration ____________________

Name on card (if different from above) ____________________

Signature ____________________

Special instructions or book inscription request: